Everyday Things With Morgan

K.J. Massey

WestBow Press books may be ordered through booksellers or by contacting:

WestBow Press
A Division of Thomas Nelson & Zondervan
1663 Liberty Drive
Bloomington, IN 47403
www.westbowpress.com
844-714-3454

Because of the dynamic nature of the Internet, any web addresses or links contained in this book may have changed since publication and may no longer be valid. The views expressed in this work are solely those of the author and do not necessarily reflect the views of the publisher, and the publisher hereby disclaims any responsibility for them.

Any people depicted in stock imagery provided by Getty Images are models, and such images are being used for illustrative purposes only.
Certain stock imagery © Getty Images.

Scripture quotations are taken from the New American Standard Bible®, Copyright © 1960, 1962, 1963, 1968, 1971, 1972, 1973, 1975, 1977, 1995 by The Lockman Foundation. Used by permission.

ISBN: 979-8-3850-1568-9 (sc)
ISBN: 979-8-3850-1739-3 (hc)
ISBN: 979-8-3850-1569-6 (e)

Library of Congress Control Number: 2023924621

Print information available on the last page.

WestBow Press rev. date: 01/25/2024

WESTBOW
PRESS®
A DIVISION OF THOMAS NELSON
& ZONDERVAN

To my daughter, Morgan.

I pray that you will enjoy reading this book to your daughters.

To my mother, who began the legacy of reading
spanning four generations. Thank you, Mom!

I want to thank my life coach, Carol Meade, who gave me an assignment one
day; without that assignment, this book would never have been written.

And last, but most assuredly not least,

I want to give my Lord and Savior, Jesus Christ,

all the glory for this effort. He is my Papa, and I adore Him.

Morgan was a very happy little girl who was very curious. Morgan's mama knew this and wanted to teach her about Jesus in everyday things.

Morgan loved to pretend while playing with her dolls. She would call them her "babies." She loved to put them in her toy stroller and take them for a nice walk.

Do you like to play with your dolls?

"Come, my children, listen to me; I will teach you the fear of the LORD" (Psalm 34:11).

One day, her mama was babysitting a friend's little girl. They decided it would be fun to take both of the little babies for a stroll together. While they were walking, the birds were out sitting on a tree limb. They were very busy just *chirp-chirp-chirping* away.

Morgan pointed to the tree and asked her mama, "Just what are those birds chirping about?"

Her mama told her they were singing songs to God, saying, "Thank you, God, for a beautiful day!" And she believed they were.

Do you like listening to the birds chirp?

"I will give thanks to the LORD with all my heart; I will tell of all your wonders" (Psalm 9:1).

Morgan's mama always remembered to tell her how much she loved her. One day Morgan's mama asked her, "Morgan, do you know how much I love you?"

And Morgan guessed, "As big as the sky?" And you know what? She was right! Morgan's mama believed that is the biggest you can love anybody, because the sky is so big, and so is God. God created the sky, and His love is all around us!

Mama wanted Morgan to know that even when she wasn't with her or when she didn't feel loved, her mama always loved her, just like God loves us.

Do you know how much God loves you?

"Blessed be the LORD your God who delighted in you" (1 Kings 11:9).

Morgan and her mama learned Bible verses together for Sunday school. This was fun because Morgan was very good at memorizing, and she loved learning about Jesus.

One of the verses Morgan had to memorize was from the book of Ephesians, chapter 4 verse 32. It says, "And be kind to one another, tender-hearted, forgiving each other, just as God in Christ also has forgiven you."

Morgan also loved to sing. She loved to sing "Jesus Loves the Little Children" because it taught Morgan how God loves everyone no matter whether they are red, yellow, black, or white.

Do you know how to sing this song?

"And be kind to one another, tender-hearted, forgiving each other, just as God in Christ also has forgiven you" (Ephesians 4:32).

Morgan adored her daddy and thought he was the strongest man in the world. She thought he was so strong that she told everyone he could lift a car, and if he wanted to, he could lift the house.

Mama taught Morgan what the Bible says about daddies. She said, "Our daddies show us a litle bit of what our Heavenly Father is like. They are strong, loving, and kind." Morgan's daddy taught her about God and the Bible, too.

"Daddies also show love by holding you in their laps and carrying you on their shoulders and letting you ride them like a horsey," she said.

Do you get to ride on your daddy's back?

"The father of a righteous child has great joy" (Proverbs 23:24).

Morgan had a very big imagination, and she loved to color pictures. One day, Morgan took her orange crayon and colored on the walls, the couch, and the carpet.

Mama was very surprised. She said, "Morgan, did you color on the walls?"

And Morgan answered, "Yes!" She was very proud of her work. But Mama had to take Morgan's crayons away for a little while, and Morgan became sad.

Mama explained to Morgan, "God's Word says for children to obey their parents." Mama loved that Morgan was creative and wanted to show her the proper way to use her imagination. Then Mama gave her a big hug.

Do you like to use your imagination?

"Children obey your parents in the Lord for this is right" (Ephesians 6:1).

Mama taught Morgan why helping others pleases God. So when Morgan visited her Mimi, she wanted to help her cook. She loved to sit on the counter and help Mimi cook her special enchiladas. She liked to help by giving Mimi the tortillas.

Once when Mimi turned around to get the next tortilla, Morgan had sneaked and put one in between her toes. They just laughed and laughed. Morgan told her she just *had* to do it! Morgan was such a silly Billy! She loved to giggle and laugh.

Do you like to be a silly Billy?

"Whatever your hand finds to do, do it with your might" (Ecclesiastes 9:10).

One morning, Morgan got up from bed, and her mama told her they were going to bake a chocolate cake and have a tea party. Morgan thought that was really special, because she had never had chocolate cake for breakfast. Mama wanted to surprise Morgan with this secret and hoped that maybe one day, if she had a daughter, she could surprise her the same way.

After they had baked the cake and set the dishes on the table, Morgan invited two of her favorite stuffed animals to the tea party. They all sat down to have tea and chocolate cake. Morgan sipped her tea and pretended her guests were eating also. They had a wonderful time! When their tummies were full, Morgan thanked her mama and said this was the best surprise ever.

Do you have tea parties with your stuffed animals?

"This is the day which the LORD has made; let us rejoice and be glad in it" (Psalm 118:24).

Every day was an exciting and fun day with Morgan. She knew that she could learn about God while having tea parties with her stuffed animals, taking walks with her mama, and playing with her babies. Soon Morgan was getting ready for school, where a whole new world of adventures would begin!

THE END

Bible Memory Verses

#1 "Come, my children, listen to me; I will teach you the fear of the LORD" (Psalm 34:11).

#2 "I will give thanks to the LORD with all my heart; I will tell of all your wonders" (Psalm 9:1).

#3 1 "Blessed be the LORD your God who delighted in you" (Kings 11:9).

#4 "And be kind to one another, tender-hearted, forgiving each other, just as God in Christ also has forgiven you" (Ephesians 4:32).

#5 "The father of a righteous child has great joy" (Proverbs 23:24).

#6 "Children obey your parents in the Lord for this is right" (Ephesians 6:1).

#7 "Whatever your hand finds to do, do it with your might" (Ecclesiastes 9:10).

#8 "This is the day which the LORD has made; let us rejoice and be glad in it" (Psalm 118:24).

About the Author

K. J. Massey is a health coach who works with clients to help them lose weight and improve their health. She serves at her church in the kids' ministry, and she loves to be outdoors playing tennis and kayaking. She and her husband, Tim, enjoy time with their dog and golfing together, and they have been married for more than forty-five years. They have two granddaughters, Mallory and Addie, and their mama is the very Morgan in this book.

Printed in the United States
by Baker & Taylor Publisher Services